FLOWERS of SULPHUR

Mario Petrucci

FLOWERS of SULPHUR

ENITHARMON PRESS

First published in 2007
by Enitharmon Press
26B Caversham Road
London NW5 2DU

www.enitharmon.co.uk

Distributed in the UK by
Central Books
99 Wallis Road
London E9 5LN

Distributed in the USA and Canada
by Dufour Editions Inc.
PO Box 7, Chester Springs
PA 19425, USA

ISBN 978-1-904634-37-9

British Library Cataloguing-in-Publication Data.
A catalogue record for this book is available
from the British Library.

Typeset in Albertina by Libanus Press
and printed in England by
Antony Rowe Ltd

for Carmela

ACKNOWLEDGEMENTS

I am indebted to: the Poetry Society's *Poetry Places* scheme for supporting my Imperial War Museum residency; the Royal Literary Fund for fellowships at Oxford Brookes University; the Arts Council England (London) 'Grants for the Arts – Individuals' Fund.

Thanks are due to the editors of the following publications and web sites: *Acumen, Ambit, Charnel House, Citizen 32, emagazine, Envoi, Frogmore 50, Illuminations, In the Company of Poets* (Hearing Eye, 2003), *Leviathan Quarterly, Listening to the Birth of Crystals* (The People's Poet, 2003), *Literati Magazine, Literature Matters* (British Council), *Magma, Obsessed With Pipework, Orbis, Other Voices* project (www.electrato.com), *Poetry Nottingham, Poetry Wales, PPQ, Rattapallax, Resurgence, Scintilla, Seam, Smiths Knoll, Social Alternatives, Soundings, Stand, Tabla Book of New Verse 1999* and *2001, The Bloody Quill, The Blue Nose Poetry Anthology, The Interpreter's House, The New Writer, The Real Survivors Anthology* (Sixties Press, 2006), *The Spectator, The Tall-Lighthouse, This Film Is Dangerous: A Celebration of Nitrate Film* (FIAF Book of Cinematic Verse, 2002), *War, Literature & the Arts* (USA), *Writing the Bright Moment* (Fire in the Head, 2005), www.poetsagainstwar.org.uk, *Yellow Crane*.

BBC commissions and broadcasts include: the World Service; National Poetry Day (*Late September, 2001*; BBC.co.uk / news); 'Kit and the Widow Cocktails' (Last Night of the Proms, 2004); Radio 3, 'Sunday Feature' (for *terranauts*).

Competition first prizes went to *India* (The New Writer, 2003), *Sinistra* (Kick Start, 2002), *Negatives* (Bridport, 1999), *Boxgrove II* (London Writers, 1998) and *Light* (Frogmore, 1996). Z was commended in the 2004 National Poetry Competition.

*

My thanks to colleagues and friends, whether they took a spanner to a single line or rolled up sleeves to the entire manuscript: Moniza Alvi, Roselle Angwin, Alix Burack, Martyn Crucefix, Tim Dooley, Sarah Dudman, Philip Gross, Tom Jones, Frances Nagle, Rosemary Norman, George Szirtes; companions at the Blue Nose workshops (particularly Sue Hubbard, Denis Timm, Brett Van Toen) and at Oxford Brookes University (Vicki Bertram, Helen Kidd, Rob Pope, Henry Shukman, plus members of Alison Waller's workshop); Jane Duran and Michael Donaghy (for consultations on *Three Mile*). To Brennos and Anne: thank you, for such showerproof support, for the sheer tonnage and grace of your involvement.

CONTENTS

Keeper of the Kilogram

CHEMISTRIES

Night Flaw	13
In Touch	14
Ark	15
Flame Juggler	16
Bunshop	18
Elisabetta	20
Insides	21
Forno	22
Amaretti	23
Sinistra	24
Z	26
Mr Hayes	28
After School	30
Volunteer	31
Reckoning	32
terranauts	33

HABEAS CORPUS

Nape	39
Stay	40
Miss Patience Muffet	42
India	44
Almost Awake	46
Tonsillitis	47
Stroke	48
Wanted to say something about grandfather	49
Opening the Graves under Spitalfields Crypt	50
Opened	51
Light Stitching	52
Anechoic Chamber	53
Lessons	54
Last Words	56

FOOTAGE

Secret	59
Boxgrove II	60
Light	62
Three Mile	64
Spaghetti Westerns	66
Pyre-Watchers	68
Hobo	70
Tailback	71
Orders of Magnitude	72
Request	73
Airfix	74
Negatives	76
The Liberation of Berlin Zoo	77
Soldier, Soldier	80
Late September, 2001	81
Footage	83

"... onward to the tall city of glass
that is the laboratory of the spirit."

R. S. Thomas

KEEPER OF THE KILOGRAM

Measurements take time. Preparation.
Servos purr away the case – bathysphere
of solid copper, forged for the atmosphere's
buoyant ocean. Thick edge of the viewport
has the green of fathoms. All round him
the muted form of basement brickwork, sealed
beneath cellophane gloss. Attention: focussed
on the squat cylinder, its tough burnish.
Now he must be careful. Places it
on one pan; working mass on the other.
Touches neither. Takes half an hour to brush dust,
microflakes of skin, aside. A sprinkling
of pollen would change everything – one
speck of sputum slide him back to first base.
Messy impostor, among the constancies
of nature. Case descends. Eddies subside.
He waits.
              This microcosmic weather
must settle to the utter still of noon,
metres above. He corrects for the upthrust
of air; humidity, temperature,
pressure. The CO_2 he himself
has contributed. He lowers the knife-
edge fulcrum: a quartz razor closes the last
thin millimetre to a mirror square
of sapphire. Sets the balance swinging.
The light-spot on the far stretch is a slow,
slow pendulum that marks mass. His gaze, steady
as bedrock. And exactly one minute
for each glide of that tiny full moon
to extremity on its sky-blue wall.
In which time, the pre-war eyelash will at last
dislodge from the internal housing. Fall
serenely towards gross error.

CHEMISTRIES

'Say it, say it, the universe
is made of stories, not of atoms.'

Muriel Rukeyser

NIGHT FLAW

Hard-down on your street it squats – each
smash of light, the <u>thunderous grab right</u>
on its heels with hardly time to count to
One – tonight autumn breaks her back
across your eaves, shudders panes as with
fingers laced to one strange hand we part
nets on a world – freed of intentions,
its canopy grazing your backboned semis,
that burn of photocopiers splicing air as air
grows thick and resinous, chill as cream
on skin, spilling in at your open sash from
sky's orange-pink cornea whose capillaries
run quick pulses of electric blood
      – seized, possessed
of so much witness.

IN TOUCH

That ocean divides. Yet the yeasts on my toes
have stowed away on yours – at the heel

of a day crammed with doings, shoe-snug,
they waft up to you our distinctive tang.

There's a suspicion in the breath I catch
single-handed, just after brushing my teeth,

of that must my tongue first muscled in on
when our kissing strayed across the Channel

and a hybrid gas hibernates in my warp
of sheets, in my nightclothes – a smell that's

somewhere between us, nuzzling to my body
warmth, or nosing the weft of denim that

spanned four shoulders of our lumbering
golem through hugger-mugger November nights.

Those secret hordes make us a common host:
cling, spawn, multiply in and under these skins –

our bodies' soft continents.

ARK

With you here, I had a zoological time.
At the sink I slobbered your nape

with bloodhound kisses, paw on each shoulder.
Was all meerkat for your key in the door.

In the shower I'd be robin, cheeping
my heart out from a steam-basted chest.

Under dawn duvets I was squirrel-whiskered –
fossicked and dug you, all scratchy-toed.

Cold evenings, iguana, I'd slow-lick
lips, all-foured around your trunk.

And when you said I was your man
I brayed so they heard it in Bosotoland.

Now you're gone, they cower under lock and key.
Come back. Bring out the animals in me.

FLAME JUGGLER

(Leicester Square)

Such trenchcoats of effort she sweats in.
All afternoon that methylated blue

pulled tight into loops about her,
each gasoline skittle a rotor constrained

by her law, then *There* – under each pit,
clenched in teeth, between the legs.

Wrists peppered with soot. The *slop*
slap of endless metal against palm, eyes

returning the flicker like tossed coins –
those pewter and copper moons she thrills

from our grasp with devastating gravity
only to ping weakly by the kerbside saturn

of her hat. Its crushed brim, its
reek of meths. Hers, a life of parabolas

where nothing must collide. Her children –
lost in the twirl of a baton. She drops

only once, trying the impossible – all
four abandoned to the air, the whites

of her eyes rolled up to God, hands poised
in utter trust of trajectories.

                    Oh by all the Gas Giants
I wish she'd come home. I'd sponge off

the stink. Watch her slick spread
through suds, sink each raft of froth

to make my bath the dark deep of a loch.
I'd work each elbow, forearm, those

liquid fingers – but no. She's still
on a roll. Still all at one with herself.

BUNSHOP

Startle-eyed, me and she, in the bunshop
where fourth-formers tried on cool

like over-sized blazers, lipsticked
with doughnut sugar and jam, and girls

gave little swivels in checked skirts,
dipping liquorice in lemon sherbet.

I peered into the deep pile of her mop,
saw white crumbs of scalp. Smelt sulphur.

First detention ever, for using perchlorate
to singe her initials in benchwood.

Mr Grant: pissy lab coat, jaundiced
coot, grimace in a dough of face, thread

of custard forever stranded between
dummy lips – *Use your loaf boy.*

Too late. Hovering behind the homework
each night: her marooned complexion, those

small white teeth. That sulphurous perfume.
End of term. Her hand in my pocket

my éclair in the other, I blew it.
Three stupid words. *I'm a Catholic.*

The shop – a delicatessen now. The school
long since converted. Yet, hanging round

the drains, something still of Mr Grant
and her – that whiff of coconut mat

in her blouse, his nicotined lard of finger
and thumb, the spatula pinched between

dipped in the tart yellow of that test tube:
Make a note boys. Sulphur. Flowers of.

ELISABETTA

It was in the haystack, where chickenshit flaked
like chalk and hogs blurted rich gas, that you

took my chin, perched it on your thumb, then
kissed me – *like a sister* you said – but *one day,*

you mimed, *one day, just wait.* And in the field
as sweat hung from your chin (a crystal drop

just before siesta that curved the light, drew in
all the sky and sun, then too fast for the eye

hurtled back to dirt) you all but sang: *I have
something. Wait.* And the peach from your apron

was pale velvet on a stone, nearly green, yet
I ate it to please you.

                         But I was eight, you twelve,
and we'd have to wait till I climbed, head bent,

out of my sister's Cortina to see you with that
cauldroned stomach, arching your back under

the vines, arm casual around his dark waist
so that a wire twisted in my gut, though I

wasn't sorry, I was English now, and this
the country where chickenshit got zigzagged

in the treads of my Green Flash and pigs stank
and the smile drooped from your ripened face

when my gaze froze on your thumb hooked
in his belt.

INSIDES

I was hurried past, straining for a glimpse
of smoothed counterpanes, secret
arrangements of furniture. Grandma
hacked hens in the yard, threw back
gizzards for the rest to squabble over –
eyes glazed, beaks wobbling blood,
mid-July pulling its white haze
over everything – so that I snuck
back down the marbled corridor, right up
to the crack, to look, to see a strip
of him as never seen: wet with himself
the untanned tide-mark across his upper arms
his belly larval white, in and out
of view, glint of hens in his eye

    – even now breath picks up
the thought of their musty privacy
pierced, oozing past the jamb where I
stand again, wading in the ancient cool
that spills across marble, their bed
empty – but Christ's eyes still following
from the wall, pointing to the heart
the raw pecked open heart.

FORNO

Hens paddled dust, panting. A mutt in its kennel
was a dropped sack. We swilled warm cola from outsize bottles,
our cheeks sticky, waxing as fast as we wiped.

Great-uncles under the fig tree – the stiles of wicker
chairs too small for their arses – got stampeded from their pool
of cigar sweat.   Troop of cousins, we tucked

hanky squares under the backs of our caps, legionnaired
across fields rippling with noon where kamikaze bugs took us
for supertankers of sap. Bites came up like pink yolks –

flushed red ants right into the chafed angle of our balls.
Tables were a threshing of flies. Each window framed a face.
We let buttocks squish together as we paraded past,

plimsolls squelching. Raided vineyards for grapelets,
sliced limes into spoked wheels, mouths yawning for the rusted
zip they dragged across our gums, to bring a sharp

world to tongues – so that trigonometry was no more
than an ache far off, our flesh fruiting towards Roman brown,
limbs yielding to the scoops of our grandparents' arms.

AMARETTI

Toadstool tops. Two. Cracked as nana's old
knee sore. And you launched one: thumb-spun
higher than a dollar – your mouth – that catpink
ridge-beam waiting; barely budged your chin to
grind it like a roof tile; offered the other, pathetic
as a button on your outstretched palm. And I
snatched it quick as a whisker, bit, felt my tongue
melt caverns deep inside, release its acrid-sweet
almond adultness –
                        which I dribbled out in spite
of the almost-shake of your loaf, the high arches
of your brows. Then you tunnelled the wrapper
between fingers to roll a joke, a giant's
cigarillo from air's tobacco; stood it
end first on ma's stainless tea tray, flicked
your flint lighter to chase the tip with flame
which seeped downwards, filled my head
with burning –
                        until, at the last,
it wobbled, transfigured, a ganglion
of desire there, rose up into our cathedralled
Italian stairwell: willed wisp of your making
who stood, an edifice of father frowning
his gargoyled wonder into mine, our wish
held up by ash, all trembling, climbing
into hallowed space.

SINISTRA

Every kid in our street knew if you dug deep enough
you'd break, spitting dust, into everything elbow
over arse. Kangaroos with red boxing gloves.

Still, your self would be the wrong way up, downside-
upness breathing out from the hole you'd made
like a gas. But left and right? – all the same.

Me, a small bewilderment on the pavement, at attention
for my dad – *This Eass, this Wess. Why you no
understan?* Sir sneering: *Even apemen knew sky*

from dirt. Buy a bracelet, sonny. I'd pick at one hand
to make a sign: its healing back always forgot.
I looked to my indifferent body – each shoulder

a smooth white bulb. Nowhere to turn. Grandma waking
in the ward, screwing her wedding band onto the
wrong claw. The slap I got, crossing myself

the Protestant way. Father Giovanni perched in his pulpit
flapping me towards damnation with a black wing.
That uncle who'd squeeze his eyes shut to imagine

– what? His biased heart? Which way he'd pick up
a knife? Thought I'd left them behind – till once,
put on the spot, tired time opened on that

boy in me, flustered by Geography, hurrying his map
onto my globe of brain: this way for Ireland, that
for Bosnia. My eyes, wide. And life streamed in

as it is: the neighbour's lads falling into step, *lef'*
right lef'! The codger from No. 72, breathless
with tarmac, drilling a look clean through the world.

Z

Armstrong making the moon, was z. Giving that chicken
next door a synchronised Chinese burn for sidling
his angular wishbones into our hide-n-seek: z.

Zapped, before break, your double dare to work it
into Maths. *If 4a − 4b equals 2a + 6b, what is a?*
and I said z so dead-pan Sir had to scan the board.

Word spread. We were the brothers determined
to have the last letter in everything. Even Dad,
belt aloft, demanding to know what devil we'd done

in his shed, mouthed air when (backs to the outside
toilet wall) we finally surrendered our stupendous
name and rank – then chose bed over a hiding.

We pitched our duvet tent with knees, and read; you
shook the torch like a cocktail to revive it. Till Mum
brought it all down with three dull crumps from below.

You've got balls, you grinned. But it was a year
before I sprouted my first real cock-feather – chinned
z straight at the bully without back-up, his neck

wattle-red as he came at me, arms outstretched,
to wring mine. That night, you turned coat. Flushed
at me, shot short words at what the hell I'd expected

as you continued to tease your fringe in the mirror
and for God's sake wasn't I *just a bit too old?*
Your bedroom smelt of Elvis, and with those

few words z span away black as vinyl, became instead
that lingering the end-of-song guitar starts into
just before it fades to crackly nothing.

MR HAYES

How could we predict that moment
twelve full minutes into his clockwork timetable
with someone burbling he must have died or

something when his door swung open
to frame him plainly not hearing Chesterfield
relax those stupid twangs of ruler as we primed

for the usual bollocking for gathering noise
like an incoming storm – but he simply walked
quarter speed behind a nebulous hearse of thought

stood before us scanning the benchtops
as though seeking there the one impossible star
through pupils thick with focus and found

at fault – his face reverberating
all its parts to some distant force
bottom lip hued suddenly with petroleum

and all his precious laws on the brink
in the way that middle button of his labcoat
had been left undone as he nearly almost not quite

breathed some great word into that
distilled void his shaking had made and
the purity of the empty blackboard remained

behind him like a window onto the last night
of the world and our classroom became a space
lightened as if by a wind-felled tree because

Mr Hayes had walked in and walked out again
leaving us to teach ourselves and speculate – that
dark vein he laid between two white lessons

AFTER SCHOOL

We were a class of two
with the blank oak pews of learning behind us
and the long walls quiet
while the master ran through the question

and no thwack of willow
dimmed through glass; just light, cramming the lab
the master unknowable in white
pondering the question, the long corridor quiet

till he remarked some aspect of the answer might
have been better dealt with . . .
but window's brilliance caught his eye, cauled him
from the paper so I had sense only

of the electron tight in its orbit
that no music from dim transistors nosed, near-extinct,
through the glass – here was all
we could know. Vacant light. An open corridor.

VOLUNTEER

Digging his trench in Durgāpur
to peer at its profile for salt
(whether millet or rice would be best)

he sees there the face of Mrs Shiva
silhouetted against third-form glass –
the gloom of a Friday mid-afternoon

closing in and the class building pressure,
seething into weekend abandon thanks
to *Old Shiver*, school pushover,

the gently-spoken one who never
reddens but talks boys round –
and he hears again that thin chuckle

hurled from the back: *Whad'ya reckon
Miss, 'bout them Yanks in Veet-Nam…?*
though he doesn't – this time – join in, just

drinks the long look she settles on him,
that wordlessness in her brown face
now older than the world.

RECKONING

(Cassino)

Nonno, that night you
led me right up the garden
to your deckle edge of meadow,
the distant bulb dim as moonlight.
Look, you said.   The field
was black.   Beyond – black water.
You relaxed those marbled fists
to rake an invisible horizon.
On one side, us –

       on the other
Her. You think your life
is yours? An inflexible finger
jabbed at soil. *No more cousins*
than She allows. She gives:
She takes. When I am gone – you
slit your throat with a thumbnail
– who will bury their
hands in Her?

terranauts

(dig: Renny Lodge, Newport Pagnell)

how timely they work
squatting in excess gravity
moved carefully with rehearsed

ease under flared suns of
sodium near-cosmic in
mist where turf h-

eaves history & ro-
     man lemons once rolled b-
         right auguries in holds of new

     forest cargoed with bronze
& copper dowries

too easily un-
     locked this *terra*
         sigillata – far too

       light that hamlet sleep
    dreaming ley lines of hu-
man blood now blind to

economics over-arching
     its iron bridges the way
         ribs might cage those

       bogged chests of peat-
    made men or hospitals of
clay be sunk beneath these

feet in land that is all outer
      space & star-deep with china
            -chip constellations oppo-

            sing / conjoining martial
      tile & pagan cobble or
blush-sudden terracotta
                              &

while most only dig to
bury these instead s-
ink horizons &

resurrect trenches
where one nurses a lung-
ful of smoke & another snow-

shoed with gley tilts some
brown half-mug of
steam as each

trowelhand b-
      rushes gently a vow
            -el here   word there   with

                  hands throat-soft &
            trained not to shatter
but only unscramble or

      make hierarchy of
            hieroglyph matter
                  whose code w-

            hose syntax whose one *la*
          -nguage is blood-streaked
yolk of brain

&

trained also never to point
-lessly shatter i watch
each word of

bone glass iron
        eased free & hardly
                blaming tools am

                        placing it   sizing it   ex
                -amining the finish &
        faint curvature of

it as if it were jig-
        sawn part of co
                -smic egg

                                ah as late light

fails i watch gray air solemnly
preserve its stillness – till
i too dig – dig this

air to honour fra
-gments – sign up for fitting
words with all cracks showing – as

these do who swim the soil first
to unlock then piece together
some future – & thus am

bound by per-
collating word to
take me to fields at death

of morning – to walk at gentle
pace of earth on ice-
rink time &

bury there under
little tuft with a little
sand one round fresh egg

of sound

HABEAS CORPUS

'A person doesn't die when he should
but when he can.'

Gabriel García Márquez

NAPE

I am a suggestion
between workings of brain, the solid ridge
of spine – a curvature
kin to breasts, hip, loins.

Almost touchable,
I tender flesh, still, in old acquaintances
who might have been
something more.

To a subtle fingertip
my nap is velvet – in some strangers
I am a lily's stem
geisha-cool.

I glow under moons
beneath the wedge-dark, am back door to eyes –
those hogs of the bone-glint,
of the brink of sharing.

Eased aside, locks
reveal me: curtain raised on my milky
opening night – or slightly bowed,
offered to the axe.

STAY

I always lace her: a husband's right to cross those ruby strands.
In Glasgow, father's stairs rose from the door in uneven heights

so the interloper's tread might trip there, raise the alarm.
I'll make like staircase of her back, a flight no lover

may decode – reverse the plait at the thirteenth eye-
hole to throw the bastard stride. Chastity belts

they say, make of locksmiths favoured escorts
– that corsetier, Alexis, comes to tea

too much. I plant a knee on her firm
lee slope, grasp her rigging, and rock

back – will complete my wife: an hour-
glass whose neck will not let time

pass, her spine a tight ship I
may steer past queen or prince

– until the whalebone creaks
with each sigh as the

last wheeze of a wreck
– breaths in shallow

draughts as if her
breast had been

brushed in the
street by

the hand
of a

strang-
l

er

MISS PATIENCE MUFFET

Afternoons in his study I squat
at the mahogany cabinet. Papa and his

rows of plump bodies. One a bruised
grape – another a spotted sultana engorged

in brandy. Some are a meeting of legs
and little else. Bristled tarantulas

light as bird-bone. Diamond-backs.
The Widow's orange hourglass.

Once, I caught him. Late with a woman –
eight limbs akimbo. Two upturned faces.

Our days spiral out from morning's
brown-paper packets: India, Indonesia,

Australia, Tasmania. I run scissors
round the edges – plop the drowsy knots

into glass. Then the muff of chloroform.
Formaldehyde. Sulfide of hydrogen. Which

asphyxiant? They kill so differently.
How he'll wince if legs claw, snap – bit

his lip to a leech of milk when one slipped
up my skirt. I giggled. Kept it alive a week.

But he's going. Doctor says he's to stick
to pap. The same as them – those

sots of hair that toboggan the bathtub
then tickle for air between my palms.

Each day his lips are laid with more
purple eggs. Tonight the jaws dribble

and botch at what I bring him. Whey,
soft balls of curd.   But he can't

eat – says the pain, the pain is
sucking him out. *Patience*, he whispers.

I take the largest wad of cotton,
step up to the bottle. Twist

the stopper from its slender brown
neck. In the water of his eyes

my hair is a clot of spiders.

INDIA

The wound was sleek –
black as a pike-hole.
I should have died.

But she, all bangles
and impregnable eyes,
spent a week among my

cells. At her shrug
my fibres leapt to
weave, regroup.

Deep in night's
bolt-hole the crisis
came. Slack over white

enamel I drooled blood
and sputum in slow
sheets. *I'm not*

sure I'm not
dead, I lied.   She
entered my injured sleep

crazed my porcelain skull
with fever. Now I can
loom on a cane.

Sometimes, half-
blind with noon, I'll
see her across the square

stooped at a corner in
diminishing sun –
incongruent

India – all
constellations
and dust, ministering

to whoever must be there.

ALMOST AWAKE

It'll be that kidney of yours
finally does you in, the one you keep on
giving a slow knuckle-dusting.

Sixty years clutching the wrong end
of every sticky English sentence. Still
unable to grasp – *It's not unpleasant.*

Your patient eyes, drawing *carissimi*
from their four corners of work
to sit with you, give TV face value.

That day, you'll be in your element
of bed and priest, candled Madonnas
making you a grotto of old ways.

There'll be the aunts who talk
too loud at funerals. Uncles
whose glancing conspiracies betray

they'd rather be playing cards
downstairs.   You'll make dead
sure you gave them each a word to be

getting on with – until you signal
that blood's inner circle should
tighten, and I'll have to hunch

to procure your whisper, shrivelled
yet whole. Given from
the stripped tree, a last leaf.

TONSILLITIS

In the back of your throat
histories repeat. Silly – but it
stopped your breath. Even at your age

they operated. Now you lie there
spooning cool oysters of advice down
my neck, gritty over the old wound.

Family arrive, identical with flowers.
Take turns to list the various ways they lost
some small part of themselves. The rest of you

will compensate of course – your taste
develop unusual range, ears burn uncannily
in almost digital detail. Yet, by and by,

something will crop up they can't cut out.
Then that soft bulb in our gullets will
ghost back from childhood, in awe

of a priestess of aspirin and lemon.
Again, our faces pink and fluid – that look
of disbelief, unable to speak.

STROKE

You're a perfect likeness of yourself. But that
clot knotted your brain, a dark fertilisation.

And though you blinked and breathed where you lay face-
up on the kitchen floor – your beige enamel bowl of eggs

overturned on the tiles – even though you looked at us
and blinked, you were gone.   Four minutes without

oxygen. All it takes to discharge a lifetime.

I dream that beige bowl. Watch it surface through the tiles
upturned – like some mother-god of chaos, crazed

and chapped, simply unbroken, acolytes splashed in its wake.
In daylight now you shuffle, chew. Sometimes even hum

a few notes – wind-chimes in the blank doorway of your head.
Drift around the house rehearsing the one track.   Flesh ghost.

Perhaps, somewhere, your yolk's intact. Breakfast, we watch you
crash the top off a soft-boiled.   Natalia points –

That's the way she did it, when she was alive.

Wanted to say something about grandfather

how one white afternoon under the vines
he stripped a cucumber with his penknife, and offered –
but my lecturer told us: *the edifice of consciousness*
needs a scaffold of knowledge

– though my grandfather said
nothing, just walked ahead beneath a bladderwrack of figs
whose rinsed greenish light made me gasp for brilliance
then to a cove of starfish leaves

where he speared some underwater
spiculed thing – a creature that had, it seemed, never
proper sun – and pared it, alive, to near-greenness
in hands cured to leather

by cigar smoke, the earth;
yet in me, still, that bloodless child – winks
at the one full-lit dapple finding my face, at his need
to shave a rind, strip by

translucent strip, holding its last
wet film up to light – that's it: grandfather making light
of the knowing in his eyes – how he saw in me days broad
as a noon-lit road where I see

only a narrow past: that he held out
this – his grandfather's seed – nerving that flesh, running
its length like a glyph through rock – each time I slice
watercolour stars or strike

a salad's strange mint of coins.

OPENING THE GRAVES
UNDER SPITALFIELDS CRYPT

Dull green, it glows – toy skull
made cupreous by the stewing of coins.
A century's suck through the boy's closed eyes.

In the tilted casket's bottom half
a second survivor sags. Head and forearm
alone, crystallised from her own black liquor.

The third has grown a peroxide shock –
lidless stare that yanks the researcher back
from the fumy light of his open door, from the face

of one just about to get the joke.

OPENED

i.m. Carmela Petrucci

We were a family of umbrellas – huddled there
in a seizure of black against the grave's fluorescent fake grass,
hunched in that treacherous strip of light between
cloud-cast and ground unzipped, the Father half-sombre, tight-

lipped under his double-decker brolly as endlessly
he crissed and crossed a squeegee-bottle our-lady-of-lourdes as if
She might out-mourn the sky.   So hard it rained
earth moved – making old adversaries link arms for safety as we

tested the brink with one foot, patent shoes puffed
to orange slippers of clay as we splayed down the camber, danced
almost in our wholesale slither to that bright hole
while behind the Father, his drip-feed Latin, had reared overnight

an excavator's range of clag, each scoop scarred
in triplicate grey as if by God's own fork. The heavens closed
that day, hurried us back to limousines' steamed
enclosures, shoulder-pads and Brylcreem pearled with droplets,

not one of us bearing a lungful longer that portal
too freshly exposed, its lip so glistened – so wanton – that none
it seemed got close enough to say with conviction
that she hadn't been lowered forever, that she'd ever touched bottom.

LIGHT STITCHING

Or you, father, pointing down to a Sicilian harbour –
its dark pincers compressing an eye-glass
of water

Or my skin, watered down by a lifetime out of your sun
yet thick and dark through our blood's long curing
in white light

Or your silhouette, insect-strange on the black breast
of a Northumbrian hill, our kinship of shape lost
in the white flood-down
of summer

Or that sequoia glade whose green we drank: a tall glass
where dark sank as heavier spirits do, and stirred leaves
made a white effervescence
of sunlight

Or you, black and white, slumped in that wicker chair
mourning your father, steeped in a kitchen's shadowless
fluorescence, toe-caps scuffed grey
by the glare

Or rain, elsewhere, as white horizons laddered with dark –
rain as fault-lines slanting the light – till, here, resolve
the first cold drops, steaming on your curved
back of earth

ANECHOIC CHAMBER

To leave the crooling of the lab, its liana
cables, for the anechoic cave, you have first
to unpick the code of runes and ciphers,
face the steel-lined concrete door, turn the handle
from hyphen to comma, and swoon hard back –

then to be greeted by a fairyland
of soft ice-cream cones: plastered to the walls,
to the ceiling, all point-inwards, dense enough
to stir the child in a scientist.
That first cry is dulled. Clipped.

When father died, I found myself there
after hours. I switched off the lights, heaved
that door shut, squashing a beam of moonlight
into itself. My eyes groped at the braille
of true blackness, their cones as useless

as the voice now dumb in my head, or that rod
he raised when pushed. I survived
a minute, in signal absence. Listened
to the turbine throb of my brain, my heart
slowing down.

LESSONS

Easy for me, your son,
youthful lungs trawling in one sweep –

cigar smoke, omelette,
the girl next door.

One day I told you
how in physics we'd calculated a cough holds

billions of atoms Galileo
inhaled. It took a full

week for your retort –
as always, off the nail. *Must be I've used it*

all then. From Siberia
to Antarctica – from slack-

pit to spire. That's
why each draw's so, so bloody hard.

Your drenched face was me,
silenced. Had to catch you

last thing, at the foot
of your Jacob's Ladder, ascending to the one

bulb of the landing
toilet, to tell you

I'd checked with sir.
You can't use it all, I piped, *not in a hundred*

million years. You'll get
better. Just wait and see.

Mouth bluish, a slur
suspended over your chest. Fist white

on the rail. You said
Don't hold your breath.

LAST WORDS

What were they? you ask.
What? What did he say
exactly?

Truth is, I couldn't hear.
Though I leaned so far
the blood

in his breath made me gag.
I'll settle for that
silver beach

forty years back – his gift
of gritty ice-cream. Hand
like a socket

to the ball of my shoulder.
The way he leaned
so close

I thought his breathing
the sea. *Good boy*
he told me.

FOOTAGE

'You have to hurry if you want to see anything.
Everything is disappearing.'

Paul Cézanne

SECRET

There's a blackness
in the underbelly of a cloud
brings light to attention

A slide of ivy
at the cliff's edge, shorn like electrics
by a recent fall

The boot at the wayside,
eyelets laced with grass, its
sagged foot of inner dark

A toadstool rising –
bared knuckle from newly
disturbed earth

A walk to the elbow
of a river, light meeting water
like armour, or a sword.

BOXGROVE II

A boy, knee-deep in gravel
fossicking for coins, unearths
your flint nest of chips. Balks
at your huge mushroom of skull.

You have been there so long
our spines have had time
to straighten and stretch.

What we would give
for flesh on your scoured tibias.
Those tiny saddles of talus.
We fingertip fractures

vital as cat's tongue. Measure
your gruff overhang of brow – overkill
for its bloated walnut brain.

That rag stomach contains
what was on your mind –
though you could barely say it,
cortex dim as a 20 watt bulb.

You squat in shingle, still
trying to think. Skeletons
of voles curl about you

intricate as the insides
of a watch. Someone
is sounding your pate
with a silver hammer.

We extrapolate your upturned
wok of abdomen, deduce its longer
colon – that our gut must have

recoiled with the ice, slow-wormed
back into itself.   In return –
aspic intelligence: our crania
swelling with each shivering delivery.

LIGHT

It puffed up our brains –
a bicycle-pump pressure down rubbery cords.
One hundred and eighty-six thousand
miles per second.

Dolphin has no such constancy,
hears like soup. Its grey-blue steel
jerks into air, makes children gasp.
Dolphin hoops the water – each leap
equal to its aether.

On the west coast I dug
for potatoes. Light there took its time
to gather, took time to roll in
its hard-earned pillows of dark.

Our Enlightenment boys
ply the radioactive, black-goggled
in the bomb-burst. They squint past embers
at the rim of the universe, urgent
for the one dark thing.

Already they catch it, condense it,
flourish it across the benchtop
like a royal flush. Bounce it off the cheek
of the moon. Make it check itself –
snitch on the slightest anomaly. Back
and forth, the caged exactitude.

It's the one constant, they said.
Let us build all space, all time, all
knowledge around it.

But the dolphin. The filed
white teeth, its white life.
It has missed the tide.
The fish-mammal is beached, flesh
desiccating in iridescent decay.
Its shrill scrimshaws to the marrow.

The children think it is smiling.

THREE MILE

First I saw, a gull splashed my windshield
with feathers. Dropped a bullet-hole crack
from its beak. Wound down the window –

tasted metal in my throat. Tangy as zinc.
Home, and I had to slice cucumber over
my Joe's eyes – they were burning up

that bad. Like he'd spot-welded every fence
in the neighborhood without his goggles.
They said the lab-boys' little red needle

didn't budge that day – and they had them dials
laid out better than my dashboard. So, nothing
could've happened. It had to be in my

mind, that crazy drive. In the mind of old Jack
puking all afternoon into a cracked salad bowl –
in the mind of Jessie from the store finding

three cats together at her back door, stiff
as beef jerky. We got to talking it through
though. Could be, we did see nothing – but

it brushed us for sure. Something big and mean.
Jack reckoned it must have been that *mind*
they kept telling us about, swelling up real

fast in its stainless steel skull, swelling faster
than dough. Faster than light, maybe. That's
when I saw it. Right there in my head –

The Mind. Coming out of that melting bulb
like some drive-in movie. Almost, a face.
Not made of light though, but heat.

And those sons of bitches screened it, clear
across our town. Jesus, how I tried to tell them.
But they were chin-scratching for America –

couldn't picture it. Me, I watched that hot grin
spread. Glide on. Left them on the sidewalk
all buzzard shoulders, straining into solid air.

SPAGHETTI WESTERNS

We saw them *al fresco*, hardly different
from how we ate – everything thrown into
one white bowl under a salt and peppering
of stars, the massive improbability of rain.

Three limewashed walls and a mountain.
Seats terraced out of chalk. The gloom
at the back was rock. From rifts of stone
came giggling no priest could get at.

The projectionist was a white cable running
into a pine box. Only his elbows, working.
Everyone showed – the wrinkled, the un-
nappied – while moths made interactive sorties

arriving like flares, shedding comet-trails
of dust, to alight on a twelve-inch nose or
the shimmering A4 of the padre's dog-collar.
Shoots of lemon spread from last year to favour

one side in the action; a rupture in the plaster
wrote-in a scar for Clint no director
had intended. That scene where he braves
the unsubtitled murk and (chewing the inevitable

cigar) notes the too-quiet cicada moonlight,
made all the cicadas on our moonlit hill
edge a touch louder. Later, stumbling back
in the dark, we rehearsed the plot – brought it

home – sensing a film was more or less
a film. And though we knew nothing of velour
upholstery or carpet stairs, between Clint
and that thin air, we got the picture.

PYRE – WATCHERS

Inside my wrap of arms
you might almost be   second
flesh to my skin   yet

you breathe as an almost
corpse   while behind our complexions
ash thickens by the hour

From this bed our eyes
dock in the set's weightless
silvering   believing ourselves apart from

the herd   But tonight is BSE
raw   is smoke force-fed air
as if evolution finally broke

with its human-long trajectory   There –
watch   World and Protein conspire
to stretch their blackened shins

unable   to switch on again
life support of rib and diaphragm
Nil by eye   ear   skin

A whim   Only this telly-chart
of slow pans and sleep
to navigate our thoughts by

Could   amino acids spring
their bonds   fly separate
ways   dendrite and axon

fry their connections   DNA
unravel straight to soil
through the kind cold

guts of earthworms   Yet
bodies resist   You say
molecules in their convoys

of smoke   were people
once   Now lost in
the swirl   the drift

of sly chaos they writhe
beyond that electric pane   make
mute faces at us   Yours

grows darker   Together we lie
Wait   for something to fall
to ply the earth   again

tender as rain

HOBO

hunched against road, legs splayed
across the broken white line he

streams from cherry blancmange of cheeks – oh
see it run, easy as a washerless tap

in its long winding down tarmac, watch
blood twist a phosphorescent Amazon

clear from my office space – its infra-
red on black, its two-tone plasma-silt

intimate as semen – watch fury tremble
in that brim-full container of face

while shoppers pause and wattles jerk
for a Samaritan view – as he drips, just

drips his shocking red till it arrives
almost sweet on the dark lip of my watching,

until I have to drink, take him in, in
gulps of gaze – the juice he spits

crushed straight from that ancient fruit
he clutches at and clutches

as though one clench of chest were his
coming, too late, to the cold press

of himself.

TAILBACK

A hundred feet ahead – the motorcycle
distorted against sodium-lamped tarmac, it seemed
a melted sweet – the car gridironed into the crash barrier,
the driver sliding his face between hands and blood while
uniforms stayed cool, in touch with base, taping out
wild swerves of rubber, indulging their blue flashes
of evidence and someone close up front got out to
ask if he might help, and for his trouble received
an accompanying hand on the shoulder

while a couple of ranks back fingers
began to tap, radios came on, and curses splashed
against stoppered time as we, caught at the fading edge
of concern's spectrum, for ten whole minutes were forced
to breathe our own fumes – until a fluorescent hand waved
permission, pent-up steel was loosed, the flow jerked then
eased, the pop and crunch of glass fell quickly behind while
as if by a failure of power, and one by one, those twinned
red eyes of braking blinked shut.

ORDERS OF MAGNITUDE

One hundred thousand trillion joules
to turn an ice cap into mush

One hundred thousand billion joules
to erase a major Eastern city

A hundred thousand million joules
to run a car to death

One hundred million of the same
for Fire Brigades to reach the kitten

Ten million just to keep
December from cold feet

A hundred thousand joules for a mug
of tea – A hundred joules

for a second's worth of War and Peace
Ten to raise a hand – to lift

an average apple to the lips
A single joule to shout the command

Half a joule to pull the trigger
Just one tenth to push the button

Almost zero to have the thought.

REQUEST

Have you a poem, anything
on Kosovo?

You know –
something to capture

the mood of the Nation?
Like Bosnia?

We want to air what
an artist has to say –

something bold, but short?
By Thursday?

AIRFIX

Those millimetre men came in boxes,
sprouted in rows from plastic stems.
Had to be twisted off at the heel,

attached to their bases using pegs.
Horses at full strain – stuck down
by one thermoplastic hoof, their riders

anally inserted by a stud at the saddle.
Thought nothing of it, the heavy-sweet
perfume of glue galloping through my brain.

Looking at my troops I knew something wasn't
right, but couldn't make anything stick
for good, except the cap to its tube,

though I rewrote history after school –
Cherokee scalping 1st Panzer Division,
cowpokes stampeding the Iron Duke. Once

I repelled a Roman Empire from the shores
of our pond with a single Spitfire.
I left snipers overnight in the throats

of nasturtiums, secreted grenade-throwers
in petalled explosions of zinnia –
just to keep the garden on edge.

It took hours to array them, seconds to
annihilate. But glue was all I needed then
after a double-handed mine – and broken men

were dabbed together, stood between
two books by the fire until morning
returned them, upright and true.

NEGATIVES

(*Photographic Archive, Imperial War Museum*)

You'd think an unnamed General, on glass,
safe? But some Private washed him improperly
in the Somme, so he just keeps on developing.
His forehead bluff with craters.

Gelatin's no better. Too warm, too moist,
and there's a precise species of mould ready
to bombard its plane. Vegetation's lowest order
reclaims these trenches.

Even envelopes rebel. Acid leaches
from each pore, syringes out the silver
to spatter the illusion or roll time's gas.
The stumbling, enveloped again.

Sudden heat is fatal. Wipes each
slate clean, each little foursquare pane.
Images peel. Their quantum flakes detach –
a miniature snowstorm in black.

So it's all kept cool. Under control.
In the darkroom's Martian light another face
gets half-way saved. The General's two
pressed dimensions, dying to explode.

THE LIBERATION OF BERLIN ZOO

"Whenever you see a green space in Berlin be very suspicious."

A shell ladders the wire fence top to bottom –
skids to its middle in mud, a huge sizzling clove.
And out they stalk under wide noonlight –

wary at first, casting this way and this
with the yellow of hunger that winks
in phosphorescent coins. The cats currmurr –

a liquid that beats in their throats low and thick,
almost a cello. Movement stirs instinct –
ankles, wrists, pale exposures of neck.

Jaguar begins. Her continents of muscle
flinch. She unwinds her crouch into the convoy's
parallel herd – embraces from behind, full pelt,

a traffic policeman, his white-gloved salute
the flash of a doe's tail. In the act of being
savaged his hands signal on – and for seconds

diverted trucks respond without dent or screech.
On Tiergartenstrasse, Panther is surprised
onto its haunches by Oberkommandierender Guttmann

rounding a bend. Animal meets animal. Panther
grins – lifts a black velvet claw. Guttmann
raises a hand. And for a moment they are old

co-conspirators slapping pad to palm – before
a single swipe opens a flap in Guttmann's pot
neatly through the buttonhole, spills his coils

into winter which at last he feels, threading him.
Panther swills bloodwine. Fangs the sweet cakes
of a half-digested Limburger lunch.

Orang-utan has mounted a tram. Points back
at children, one arm trailed in a mockery of style,
chin cocked to velocity's breeze. Tonight she'll drag

knuckles right up the Reichstag steps, plant
a trained suck on the cheek of the porter. His look
will pale her into intelligence. On Potsdamer Platz

Zho crops turf. Her eyes betray a sidewise disposition
towards predators louche in the alleys behind speakeasy
and bar. Yet something is missing from the maw

of buildings – a tooth pulled from history to make
this square of sward, which Zho crops simply because
it grows, because it ranks so unnaturally green.

Last is Python. Her anvil head, by degrees,
jacks towards dim hammerings of free air, grim
to push the die-cast snout into any nest of blood.

The cold slides into her. She slops into culverts
heavy as a rope of copper – moulds to the sewers,
wraps the city in coils of intention. Develops

a rattle for Russia, a string of diamond yellows
for Poland. She winds up a tension. And Berlin ticks
inwards, becomes a city breathless, a gasp of dust

where Volkswagens are specks, circling crazily.
But there is nothing to fear. Not now. The cats
have had their fill – only pawprints lead through snow

down to the mouths of alleys. A white-gloved
claw is on the kerb. The people walk round it, pull
tight their collars. Eventually, from a windowbox

in Charlottenburg Palace, a single petal of phlox
will bear down into the shallow cup of its palm
with all the weight of a snowflake.

The opening quote is attributed to Pieke Biermann (unverified).

Heavily bombed, Potsdamer Platz was later split by the Berlin Wall.
Between 1939 and 1945, Tiergartenstrasse no. 4 was the originating
address for orders requiring the 'euthanasia' of 200,000 people.

SOLDIER, SOLDIER

Friend, everything came
together to make us upright, warm.

Hold firm – soil looking on soil.
We will never happen again.

How on earth withhold
an embrace? Or guide

the rifle-butt home?

LATE SEPTEMBER, 2001

There'd been dew. Perhaps light rain.
And a blot drew my eye to that square of white
through the kitchen window. Closer. I saw

pincer legs measure out each wire. That
pause of the abdomen before it dipped to
spot-weld each link. I took a chair outside

to stand on. I wanted to live. It let me
brush a fingertip across the brown felt
of its back, against the nap, and again till it

stalled in air, eight legs outstretched, still
as a child roused from the trance of play. Here –
the same creature I'd raise my slipper to,

hunt across carpet to end in a smudge.
I wouldn't have it in my hand. In my hair.
Yet it – she – went to all that length to snare

mosquito and bluebottle, those who might
ruin soup, drink blood. Hours. For once
I took time. Saw her target complete, strung

high between window and washing line.
How a twist of cells can work such wonder
where a poet's words don't reach. Spider

just does. Reads the angles. But not this freak
impending thunder. And I saw birds, birds
everywhere. Swooping for spiders. I feared

something might skim, unknowing, through that
hard-earned web. A swift perhaps, far too late.
I saw spider, hung in her patch of unsafe sky.

FOOTAGE

So we crashed round the bend,
We heard his weak scream,
We heard his very last sound,
And our wheels grazed his dead face.

Isaac Rosenberg

Trenchcoats bedraggled
limb-fluent behind
the flickering hair

the mad zag of a scratch.
Mist of time, literally.
Watching

That quenched hour
of afternoon waiting
for you, when people walk

like the dead, I pace
for you, I watch
like the dead

Children. Stood like stock
on grass, innocent as cows
in Red Square. But they know

the camera's eye, are still
for it, shy to it. Time
has brought blood to celluloid –

blushes these scarecrow men
who gap-tooth into camera
who waltz to silence

Yesterday. Bracket fungus.
Palace balconies scalloped
with gold. Today

collapsed by frost
into curd. As wounded walking
I walk you to the car

A man wrenches back
Falls to death in four frames
He does not fall

continuously, but as he falls
finds four selves for company
Always the same

Edge-on, a woman, facing camera
places a finger in the black wound
of her limewashed hearth

Woman. Trying to climb back
into you, into you, but only
finger, tongue, prick at a time

The large part of conflict –
standing, the drag
at the cigarette, pacing

the sudden dash of eyes
through smoke, just four frames
to fall in

For whom do I watch?
Ghost-blur on the screen
that flicks a leg, a hand?

A pony. Shock across pelt
as the thorn of shrapnel
is tweezered from shag

You push back
a boy, complete, formed right
to the thumbnail

Pat on the back. Cigar.
I don't smoke. All breath
is smoke

Men, leap into frame
swim across frame, a river
of shaggled men, walking

A press of men, dull slug
of flesh, slow ripple
of defeat

Co-ordinate animal, grey-slick
muscle, each man a scale
of the snake surging

past burst nests
that were houses, gliding,
lifting hats, smiling

to the lens, men without
teeth smiling, nursing
a bundle the size of a fist

A bundle brought in
for display   the crushed face
squeezes out its cry

who squeezes out
my cry when I've got it
so good

Commandant strolls in
and the hand at the lathe
is half a frame too keen

their grin at His arrival
half a face too soon
into camera   *Hello*

they stride me into smoke,
up to the bar, clear the old
stout bottles, part the stench

Stout bottles! cannons
that poff into men
a black crawl

of men staggered
across broken snow
like a thaw

You bend to the water
I scrub your back
You gasp into heat like a thaw

rock with my pressure as I
pace you, keep eyes on the bundle
that frets by the tub

A man lathers
another man's back. Two horses
stumble in mud.

A cow, pick-axed
through the white locks
of its forehead. Twice.

The image plants the germ
but is not the germ.
It is innocence

violate. I must watch
the men, the snake
because they show it

here in the afternoon while I
wait, in this quenched hour
that the fungus melts in

till the smoke you stumble
out of, your gasp at the child
you lift from the tub

This woman, your body,
this child yet to come
to manhood —

will we smile at camera
at the cannon, at the cannon
that is a stout bottle, will he

The counting
of legs, ranks of ankles
faces covered, chests

sunk into sludge
the ranks of legs, a horse
rearing, flaring, smells

death. Boys eager
with the shovel
to stand with the men

at this canal
that is a grave
the next corpse

flops into
casual as a father
rolling from his couch

I see the foam
brown with your rust
the tub

a canal
of rust
sunk in snow

I can see
This, yet do not
act

and the boys with shovels
look into camera
with each carcass that

rolls to final sleep
Their eyes say – *do you*
see, do you, you

eye of long
memory?   Do
you see

that?

DR ERADICUS

Dr Eradicus was a good friend.
He always kept his word. In fact,
he taught me much about words.

I remember him telling me
by the glow of his hearth
one dark earnest night

that he was on the brink
of a Great Truth. *Look up*
he said, *a long and difficult word.*

It is always described in terms
of simpler words. Pursue those
simpler words, he continued

and you shall find them defined
by stint of simpler words still.
By now I was totally absorbed.

I believe that if this process
were to be carried back, time
and again, by natural means

(an intense look entered his eye)
one would eventually arrive
at the One Word. He paused.

From this, all other words,
long and short, convoluted
and plain, could be derived

and understood. And I believe
also that if a man were ever to
uncover this Word – *he would die.*

Minutes passed. Undeterred,
the pendulum's heavy *tock*.
When at last I spoke it was

to insist that if ever he were to
find the Word, he should
tell me. He gave me

his solemn oath.